CLASSIC ROCK BANDS

THE ROLLING STONES

by Jill C. Wheeler

CONTENT CONSULTANT

Barry Faulk
Professor, English Department
Florida State University

An Imprint of Abdo Publishing | abdobooks.com

abdobooks.com

Published by Abdo Publishing, a division of ABDO, PO Box 398166, Minneapolis, Minnesota 55439.

Printed in the United States of America, North Mankato, Minnesota.
052021
092021

Cover Photo: Trinity Mirror/Mirrorpix/Alamy
Interior Photos: Terence Spencer/The LIFE Images Collection via Getty Images/Getty Images, 4–5; King Collection/Photoshot/Hulton Archive/Getty Images, 7, 45; Keystone Features/Hulton Archive/Getty Images, 11, 22–23; Popperfoto/Getty Images, 14–15; Stones Archive/Getty Images Entertainment/Getty Images, 20; Archive Photos/Hulton Archive/Getty Images, 26–27; Mirrorpix/Newscom, 29, 34–35, 76–77, 80–81; Stan Mays/Mirrorpix/Newscom, 38–39; Michael Ward/Hulton Archive/Getty Images, 42; Blank Archives/Hulton Archive/Getty Images, 48; Michael Ochs Archives/Getty Images, 50–51; Daily Mirror/Mirrorpix/Getty Images, 53; Starstock/Photoshot/Newscom, 56–57; Warren K. Leffler/Library of Congress, 60; Robert Altman/Michael Ochs Archives/Getty Images, 62–63; Mirrorpix/Getty Images, 64–65; AP Images, 67; Homer Sykes/Corbis/Corbis Historical/Getty Images, 72–73; Paul Natkin/Archive Photos/Getty Images, 85; Michael Brito/Alamy, 88–89; Aude Guerrucci/Polaris/Newscom, 92; Chris Pizzello/Invision/AP Images, 95; J. Stone/Shutterstock Images, 96

Editor: Melissa York
Series Designer: Colleen McLaren

Library of Congress Control Number: 2019954362

Publisher's Cataloging-in-Publication Data

Names: Wheeler, Jill C., author.
Title: The Rolling Stones / by Jill C. Wheeler
Description: Minneapolis, Minnesota : Abdo Publishing, 2022 | Series: Classic rock bands | Includes online resources and index.
Identifiers: ISBN 9781532192036 (lib. bdg.) | ISBN 9781532179938 (ebook)
Subjects: LCSH: Rolling Stones--Juvenile literature. | Rock and roll bands--Biography--Juvenile literature. | Rock musicians--Great Britain--Biography--Juvenile literature. | Psychedelic rock music--Juvenile literature.
Classification: DDC 782.42166--dc23

CONTENTS

CHAPTER ONE

Opportunity Knocking

Alexis Korner had a tough decision to make. The British blues musician had secured a weekly gig for his band, Blues Incorporated, at London's Marquee Club. It was a great opportunity for Korner to expose British fans to blues music. The blues had its roots in the American South, but it was now taking Britain by storm. The music style features notes played at a slightly lower pitch than the usual scale, creating a sadder sound.

Yet on July 12, 1962, Korner had an even bigger opportunity. The British Broadcasting Company (BBC) had offered Blues Incorporated a slot on its live *Jazz Club* radio

Many of the top British acts of the 1960s played the Marquee Club in London.

The Marquee Club

London's Marquee Club was founded in the late 1950s by accountant and avid jazz fan Harold Pendleton. The club held its first jazz night in April 1958. Pendleton added a regular rhythm and blues (R&B) night in 1962, which even attracted American R&B stars such as Muddy Waters.

In the early 1960s, the Marquee Club was one of the few British venues where music fans could hear the blues sound that had originated in America. The club attracted the music press as well. It became the launching pad for many famous acts, including the Yardbirds, Manfred Mann, and the Animals, in addition to the Rolling Stones. The Who, Jimi Hendrix, Cream, and Led Zeppelin also used the Marquee Club as an early showcase for their talents.

Pendleton died in 2017 at age 93. He continues to be recognized for his role in bridging unique music styles—from jazz, R&B, and blues to skiffle, folk, and psychedelic rock—to influence multiple generations of music around the world.

program. It was simply too big of an opportunity to turn down. Yet accepting the gig meant Korner would have to find a new act to fill the bill at the Marquee Club that evening.

Fortunately, Korner had an idea about which band could fill in the spot. Since founding Blues Incorporated in 1961, Korner and cofounder Cyril Davies had attracted a steady stream of fans and aspiring musicians. Blues Incorporated already was playing with young drummer Charlie Watts and pianist Ian Stewart. In addition, one of the group's recent guest singers was a young blues fan named Mick Jagger.

Guitar player Brian Jones got the members of the band together.

Korner knew Jagger had been in other bands before. He also knew Jagger had begun working with a new rhythm and blues (R&B) band. The band had started in spring of that year when blues musician Brian Jones placed an ad in *Jazz News* magazine seeking players. Jagger, along with one of Jagger's friends from school, plus several others, had auditioned for and been accepted into the new band.

Korner asked the members of the new band if they would be willing to fill in for Blues Incorporated. They said yes.

A BAND BEGINS

With the first gig coming up, the new band had to get busy and get ready. Members began rehearsing at the Bricklayer Arms pub in London's Soho neighborhood. In addition to guitarist Jones and lead singer Jagger, the band featured Jagger's friend, lead guitarist Keith Richards, along with cofounder and pianist Ian Stewart. Bassist Dick Taylor, who was another one of Jagger's friends, and drummer Mick Avory rounded out the artists who would perform that first night at the Marquee Club.

The Dawn of R&B

The term *rhythm and blues* (R&B) first was used to describe several forms of music that became popular following World War II (1939–1945). These forms developed in urban areas and became the dominant popular music form for black performers of the time. R&B draws from a range of music traditions, including classic blues, jazz, and the fast, upbeat piano sound of boogie-woogie. Music journalist Jerry Wexler coined the term in 1947 to replace the race-based terms that were being used for the category at that time.

The band borrowed money from Jagger's father to rent equipment for the show. Jones called *Jazz News* to promote the upcoming gig. The story goes that the band got its name during that call. Jones was asked for the name of the band. Desperately seeking inspiration, he found it in the work of one of the band's musical heroes, American blues great Muddy Waters. Waters's hit "Mannish Boy" features the line "I'm a rollin' stone."[1] Stewart was not crazy about the name, but it stuck. The band later changed "Rollin'" to "Rolling" on the advice of its first manager, Andrew Loog Oldham. Coincidentally, the music and culture magazine *Rolling Stone*, founded in 1967, was also named after Waters's song.

For the first gig, the band billed itself as "Mick Jagger and the Rollin' Stones." The musicians stuck to covering songs from some of their favorite artists. A handwritten set list from the night shows covers of 18 songs, including hits from Jimmy Reed, Elmore James, Chuck Berry, and Fats Domino. The band

Muddy Waters

Muddy Waters was a Mississippi-born guitarist and vocalist. Along with Robert Johnson, he is regarded as one of the most influential artists in the development of modern blues music. Born McKinley Morganfield in 1915, Waters began playing harmonica as a small child and guitar at 17. In 1943, he moved from Mississippi to Chicago and began connecting the country blues of his childhood with that city's developing urban blues. He revolutionized the blues sound by switching from acoustic to electric guitar and recording with musicians who increased their volume with electronic amplifiers.

Jagger has always been the popular lead singer at the front of the Stones.

shared the stage at the Marquee with another R&B act, Long John Baldry's Kansas City Blue Boys.

This first gig attracted about 80 men and 30 women.[2] Photographs from the event reflect an informal dress code of shapeless, utility-styled clothes, stout shoes, and square glasses. There were also a number of jazz fans with goatees. Reports from those at the club indicate that it took a while for the audience to warm up to this new band and its 50-minute American R&B set.

The band members, however, dressed more formally at their first outing than what fans would come to expect in later years. Out front was 18-year-old Jagger in a striped sweater and corduroys. Richards, also 18, was wearing a dark suit. Both men still were living with their parents at the time. Jones, 20, was dressed all in black and kept urging the rhythm section to go faster. Spectators recalled Stewart playing piano with one hand while eating a pork pie with the other.

A RESPECTABLE PERFORMANCE

Reports of the Stones' first performance regard it as a mixed success. The nervous band members were drinking Scotch and brandy, trying to calm down as they played. Bassist Taylor recalls a few catcalls from the audience in response to the band's minimal rehearsals. Stewart wrote in his diary that the band

redeemed itself in the last 15 minutes, delivering a version of "Down the Road Apiece" reminiscent of American rock and roll pioneer Chuck Berry. Then the group finished strong with Elmore James's "Happy Home."

After the gig, the musicians went to a nearby pub. They left behind a friend of Brian Jones to haul the gear out of the club and onto a bus. At the pub, the band members met Charlie Watts, who had been at the gig. Watts, who was a part-time drummer for Blues Incorporated, recalled the difference between his band and the one-night replacements. "My band was a joke to look at, but this band crossed the line," he said. "They actually looked like rock stars."[3] For their effort, Jagger, Richards, Stewart, Taylor, and Avory each received about $6.50 in today's dollars. Jones's share of the take was about one dollar more.[4]

> "I hope they don't think we're a rock 'n' roll outfit."[5]
>
> *– Mick Jagger in his very first press interview, speaking with* Jazz News

As Richards recalls, the money didn't matter. It was all about the music and the feeling of being onstage. "There's a certain moment when you realize that you've actually just left the planet for a bit," he said. "You always want to go back there. It's flying without a license."[6]

It would be years before the Rolling Stones became a household name outside of the London music scene. The band performed sporadically in London clubs in the year after its initial gig. Blues Incorporated, meanwhile, recorded an album in the summer of 1962. That album, *R&B from the Marquee*, helped ignite the blues revolution that swept the British music scene in the 1960s. It was a revolution the Stones would expand, refine, and spread around the world.

Chicago Blues

Muddy Waters was a pioneer of a blues style known as Chicago blues. The Rolling Stones favored this style. The Chicago blues style developed during the Great Migration, when some six million African Americans moved from the rural South to the urban Northeast, Midwest, and West between 1910 and 1970. Musicians among these newcomers adapted their traditional country blues sounds to the new local scene. Some utilized electrification and amplification so they could be heard over the noise at crowded clubs. Chicago blues is characterized by electric guitar, harmonica, and a rhythm section of bass and drums, and it sometimes includes saxophones.

CHAPTER TWO

Must Love Blues

Drummer Mick Avory and bassist Dick Taylor left the group a few months after the Marquee performance. Avory went on to perform with the rock band the Kinks. While Mick Jagger, Keith Richards, and Charlie Watts have served as a stable core for the Rolling Stones, other talented musicians have come and gone over the years. Two of those musicians—Brian Jones and Ian Stewart—are widely considered the founders of the band.

Lewis Brian Hopkin Jones was born on February 28, 1942, to a middle-class family in Gloucester, England. His mother, Louisa, was a piano teacher. His father, Lewis, was a

Brian Jones loved music from a young age.

Blues Sounds

One of the most distinctive styles in blues is called blues slide. It involves placing a short tube, such as the neck of a glass bottle, over one finger. That finger is then placed across the guitar strings while the other hand plays notes. This creates unique sliding and vibrating effects. Brian Jones was among the first UK performers to use it.

Howlin' Wolf, Muddy Waters, and many other blues greats incorporated the harmonica into their acts. It remains an important part of blues music to this day. It began as a simple, inexpensive instrument developed in Germany in the 1800s. Originally, it accompanied European waltzes and marches. In the hands of African American musicians in the southern United States, however, it was transformed. These musicians developed a completely different style of playing by sucking air through the instrument, as well as blowing it out. This style of playing is called cross harp. Cross harp playing results in a lower-pitched sound that more closely reflects the human voice.

music-loving engineer. He had two sisters.

Jones grew up listening to the music of American saxophonist Julian "Cannonball" Adderley. Adderley's music left Jones with a lifelong love of jazz, and he acquired a saxophone himself while still a teenager. His parents encouraged his musical interests and gave him an acoustic guitar. With the Stones, he also played sitar, organ, marimba, dulcimer, harpsichord, and oboe.

Both school and music came easily to Jones, though the structure and discipline of school was never easy for him. He was twice suspended from school. At age 17, his girlfriend became pregnant, and Jones dropped out of school as a result of the scandal.

Jones spent the next few years supporting himself with odd jobs and the occasional music gig. Following a summer of travel in northern Europe, he began to haunt the jazz and blues clubs of London. There he met other blues, jazz, and R&B musicians and began to jam with them. He also began making his own name on the club scene, attracting some fans under the stage name Elmo Lewis. By May 1962, he was ready to form his own band and take his music to the next level. He put an ad in *Jazz News*, and young keyboard player Ian Stewart was quick to respond.

PIANO MAN

Ian Andrew Robert Stewart was born on July 18, 1938, in Pittenweem, Scotland. His mother, Annie, and father, John, were both Scottish nationals who were living in Surrey, England, at the time. John was an architect who worked for the British army. Annie insisted that her baby be born on her family farm in Scotland to make sure the child could always claim to be Scottish.

That farm became an important place for the young man, who went by the name Stu. He visited his uncle there frequently, and it was on an old piano in the farmhouse parlor that Stu began plunking away. He counted boogie-woogie pianist Meade Lux Lewis, blues pianist Leroy Carr, and blues guitarist Scrapper Blackwell among his influences.

By age 23, Stewart was living and working in London. By day he was a shipping clerk for Imperial Chemical Industries. Outside of work he could be found at London's Ealing Jazz Club, one of the few venues that featured R&B music at that time. Sometimes he played with Alexis Korner's Blues Incorporated as well. It was within these circles of musicians that he met another dedicated jazz musician, Charlie Watts.

Chris Barber, Skiffle, and a Blues Revival

American blues performed by African American artists became more widely available in Britain after World War II. Blues records brought over by American soldiers found their way into secondhand music shops. Other young fans ordered the records by mail or through British jazz record labels. One blues evangelist was British trombonist Chris Barber. Called the Father of British blues, Barber set up his own jazz band. The band included a blues quartet led by Alexis Korner and Cyril Davies.

Korner and Barber both were involved in the skiffle craze taking place in Britain. Skiffle is a style of folk music with the flavors of blues and jazz. It is played on both conventional and homemade instruments, such as washboards or jugs. Skiffle started in the United States in the 1920s and hit Britain in the 1950s. Skiffle was an entry point to music for many British teenagers, including John Lennon of the Beatles and Jimmy Page of Led Zeppelin.

KEEPING THE BEAT

Charles Robert Watts was born in London on June 2, 1941, to Charles and Lillian Watts. His father was a truck driver for the London, Midland and Scottish Railway. Charlie and his sister grew up in the Kingsbury neighborhood of London.

Like his future bandmates, Watts developed an early passion for jazz and blues. He grew up listening to jazz trumpeter Miles Davis and jazz saxophonist John Coltrane. Later, he added American jazz masters Jelly Roll Morton (piano) and Charlie Parker (saxophone). By age 13, he was turning his talents toward drums and even converted an old banjo into a snare drum. His parents quickly recognized his musical talents and bought him a drum kit.

Following secondary school at Tyler's Croft Secondary Middle School, he attended Harrow Art School. In 1960, he took a job as a graphic designer for an advertising firm while moonlighting as a drummer for several local bands, including Blues Incorporated. Blues Incorporated was creating quite a following. It also was giving many new artists an opportunity to sing and play great jazz, blues, and R&B. One of those new artists was Mick Jagger.

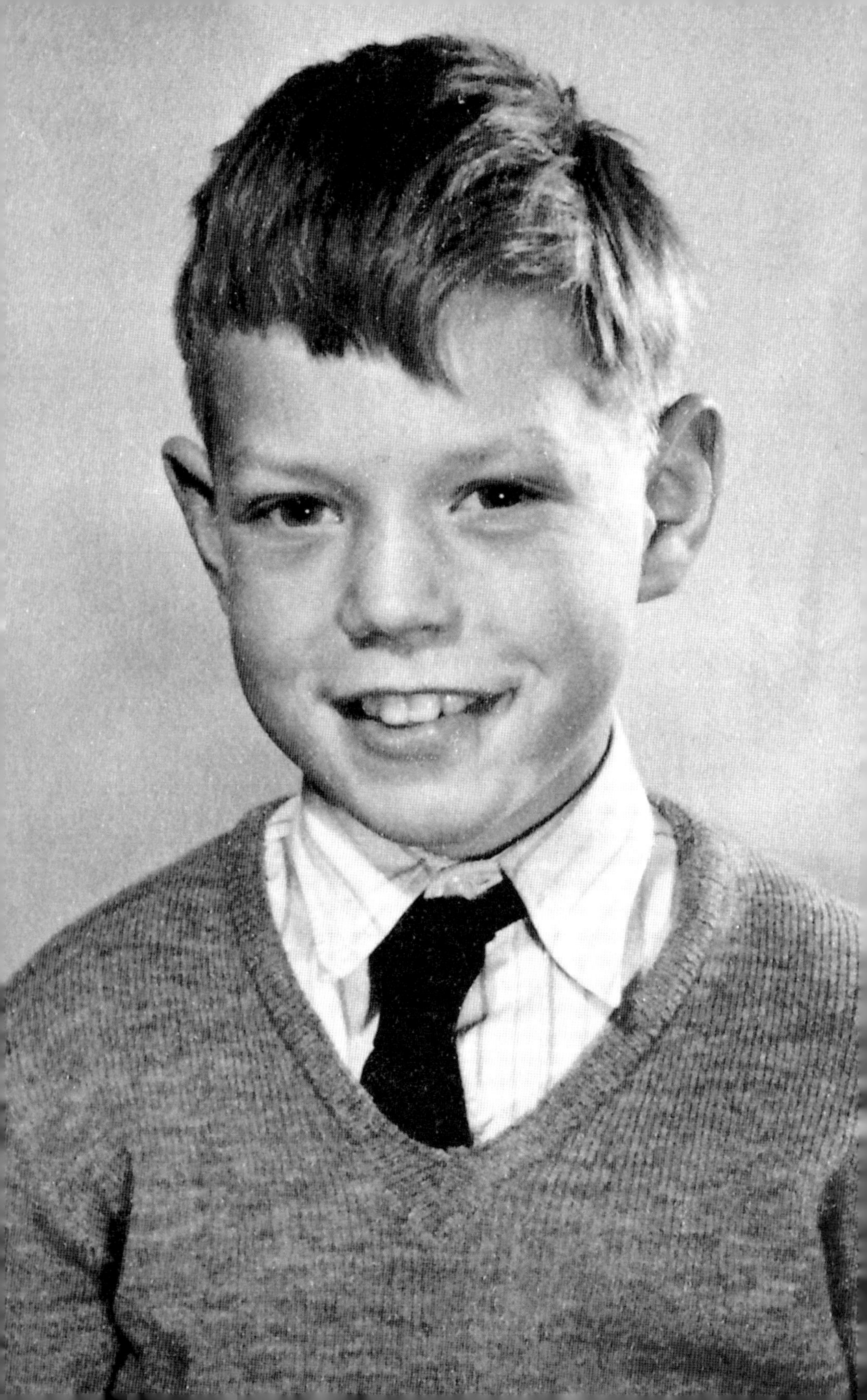

Jagger, age nine, in a school photo from Wentworth Primary School

FRONT MAN

The face of the Rolling Stones was born Michael Philip Jagger on July 26, 1943, in Dartford, England. His father, Basil "Joe" Jagger, was a gym teacher. His mother, Eva, was a hairdresser. Jagger had one younger brother, Chris.

Jagger attended Wentworth Primary School and then Dartford Grammar School, where he was a talented athlete. He recalls singing frequently as a child, including in the church choir. Joe Jagger recalled that his son could copy perfectly just about any song he heard. Like his future bandmates, Jagger also developed an early interest in blues and R&B music. He got his first guitar at age 14 and collected records by Muddy Waters, Chuck Berry, and Howlin' Wolf.

Howlin' Wolf

Howlin' Wolf was an American blues singer and composer who helped pioneer the Chicago style of urban blues. Born Chester Arthur Burnett on a Mississippi cotton plantation in 1910, Wolf began singing publicly at an early age. He served in the army during World War II, then formed an electric blues band in Arkansas after the war.

A guitar and harmonica player, Wolf was best known for his booming, guttural voice. He moved to Chicago following his first hit record, *Moanin' at Midnight*, in 1951. His nickname came from his grandfather, who called him Wolf. The Stones had a Number 1 UK hit with their cover of Wolf's classic "Little Red Rooster" in the mid-1960s.

Richards, *left*, with Jagger, answering fan mail soon after their band came together.

In 1960, Jagger enrolled at the London School of Economics. He planned to become a journalist or politician. At the same time, he and his friend Dick Taylor had started their own band, Little Boy Blue and the Blue Boys. Jagger was commuting on the

train to school from his home in Dartford one day in 1961 when he saw someone holding a Chuck Berry record on the platform. Jagger went up to the man and realized it was an old classmate from Wentworth, Keith Richards.

GUITAR LEGEND

Keith Richards was born on December 18, 1943, in Dartford, England, to Bert and Doris Richards. Bert was a foreman in a factory and Doris worked at an appliance store. An only child, Richards was especially close to his maternal grandfather, Gus, a musician.

Richards says his grandfather inspired his love of music, including playing guitar and singing. He recalls listening at a very young age to Ella Fitzgerald, Sarah Vaughn, Louis Armstrong, and more. Richards's mother presented him with his first guitar at age 15, though he had already been playing other people's guitars by that time.

Like Jagger, Richards attended Wentworth Primary School. He then went to the Dartford Technical High School for Boys. He participated in the high school choir and even sang before Queen Elizabeth II. He was expelled from high school in 1959 for skipping classes. Fortunately, an art teacher suggested he enroll instead at Sidcup Art College in London.

> "I think we realized, like any young guys, that blues are not learned in a monastery. You've got to go out there and get your heart broke and then come back and then you can sing the blues."[1]
>
> *– Keith Richards, writing in his 2011 autobiography,* Life

For Richards, Sidcup was a breath of fresh air. The music scene at the college was unlike anything he had ever seen. He spent hours playing guitar with other students. And it was on the way back to Sidcup from Dartford that he ran into his old friend Mick.

CHAPTER THREE

Getting Gigs, Collecting Fans

Although the initial Marquee Club gig was an important one for the Rolling Stones, it did not rocket the band to fame or fortune. Shortly after that gig, Jagger, Jones, and Richards moved in together in an apartment that Richards later described as "truly disgusting."[1] With little money among them, Richards recalled that they resorted to stealing from their neighbors as they rehearsed and sought out gigs.

Stewart was the only member of the band with access to a telephone, so he ended up managing callbacks and auditions from his office at Imperial Chemical. It was also Stewart who helped put together the

The Stones' lineup as of 1962: Stewart, Watts, and Wyman, *front row from left*, Richards and Jagger, *center row from left*, and Jones, *top row*

remaining core of the early Stones. In early 1963, he convinced Charlie Watts to join the band. Stewart also convinced Bill Wyman to take over the bass slot opened by the departure of Dick Taylor in December 1962.

Wyman was born William George Perks Jr. on October 24, 1936, making him the oldest of the band members. He was one of five children born to William and Molly Perks. He grew up in Lewisham, England, where he started his musical career playing organ with his father, who laid bricks for a living. A tour of duty in the British Royal Air Force exposed him to the music of Chuck Berry and Elvis Presley. He began working on his own musical career after leaving the air force and chose the bass as his instrument of choice.

Both Watts and Wyman ended up leaving better paying opportunities to take a risk with the new band. Stewart understood that Jagger, Richards, and Jones offered style and sex appeal. Yet he knew the band needed a solid base of rhythm best supplied by the older, more experienced team of Watts and Wyman.

On February 24, 1963, the Rolling Stones played what would be the first of multiple gigs at the Crawdaddy Club in Richmond. They became the Sunday afternoon house band for the venue, which was located in the Station Hotel. The Crawdaddy

Andrew Oldham would do much to shape the Rolling Stones' image.

Club was more than a pub—it was the place to be for blues fans and blues bands. The Beatles, who began their career as a skiffle band, had already played the club when the Stones began their residency.

CREATING AN IMAGE

One of the many people who caught the Stones' act at the Crawdaddy Club was 19-year-old promoter Andrew Loog Oldham. Oldham stumbled upon the band on April 23 and quickly convinced the members to hire him as their manager.

Within two weeks, he had secured a contract for the band with Decca Records.

Oldham had previously worked with the Beatles. Now he was determined to recreate the Rolling Stones to be the popular band's biggest competitor. Oldham quickly set to work with his new project. First, he added the "g" to the name. Perhaps most famously, he insisted that the band remove Stewart from its lineup. Quite simply, he explained, Stewart just didn't look like the rest of the band.

Fortunately for the Stones, Stewart took the decision in stride. He agreed to continue playing piano for the band, but only for the songs he wanted to. He also agreed to serve as the band's road manager, arranging venues and seeing that its equipment got to where it needed to be. Years later, Richards joked that Stewart, an avid golfer, would book the band rooms in hotels near the best golf courses—regardless of whether the hotels were anywhere near the concert venue.

Meanwhile, Oldham continued to shape the Stones' public image. Oldham initially had objected to the band members' longer-than-average hair. Eventually, he realized that image, coupled with their refusal to wear any kind of uniform on stage, was exactly what he needed. While the Beatles were finding success as the band loved by young people and parents alike, the Stones found a niche as the group parents loved to hate.

The Stones also began to change the way bands and fans danced. Traditionally, venues such as the Crawdaddy Club were places people went to dance. The bands performing there simply provided the music. Just as the Stones incorporated elements of other acts into their music, so did Jagger incorporate others' onstage moves. He had learned ballroom and square dances as a teenager. Yet these dances relied on having a partner. As the Twist and other solo dances crept on the scene, Jagger began to experiment with solo dancing on stage. He said he was particularly influenced by watching the West Indian dancers at a ska/blue-beat club in central London, as well as American artists Little Richard and James Brown.

Brian Jones: Fashion Icon

The Rolling Stones influenced fashion, as well as music, and Jones was the band's fashion icon. Jones wore fitted striped suits, velvet jackets, floppy hats, colorful scarves, and stylish shirts, often with fancy ties. An avid shopper, Jones also was known for having the most interesting-looking guitars in the band. Friends recall how Jones and a former girlfriend, model Anita Pallenberg, would try on each other's clothes. His famous bowl haircut was imitated around the world. The story has it that Jones never actually got a specific haircut but simply grew his blond hair to cover his forehead and ears.

THE FIRST SINGLE

In early May 1963, Oldham had the Stones in a small studio that typically recorded advertising jingles. The modest space had egg cartons on the walls for soundproofing. The band recorded a cover of the Chuck Berry song "Come On." The cover reached Number 21 on the UK singles chart as the band continued to draw crowds to the tiny Crawdaddy Club.

The success of "Come On" led to the band's first gig outside of London. This concert, in Middlesbrough, England, featured the Stones, along with British band the Hollies. The Stones followed this appearance with a UK tour in the fall of 1963, opening for Little Richard, Bo Diddley, and the Everly Brothers.

Jagger and Tina Turner

In addition to inspiration from London dancers and watching American stars from afar, Jagger's famous moves can be credited in part to R&B and pop icon Tina Turner. Turner first toured with the Rolling Stones in 1966 with her then husband Ike Turner. She recalls she did not know who the Rolling Stones were at first, but over time she got to know the lead singer who often watched her from the wings. "I tried to teach him some dances, because he'd just stand still on stage with the tambourine," Turner recalls. "He'd try things like the Pony or some hip movements backstage and we'd all just laugh."[2] Of course Jagger's dancing only improved over time.

As Richards recalls, it was during this first tour that something changed. To that point, the Rolling Stones had considered themselves first and foremost a blues band. What the members realized was that they had become pop stars to a host of exuberant young female fans. Sometimes they could barely hear their own music over the screams of fans. Sometimes they performed behind chicken-wire fencing as a safety measure. Other times, riots broke out, including when the Stones played in Dublin, Ireland, in September 1965. Fans rushed the stage just 12 minutes into the concert, abruptly ending it. The frenzy became known as "Stone mania."[3]

Like Beatlemania, Stone mania was a reflection of the times. The band was born and became popular during a period of great cultural change. Its fans came from a generation that had not directly experienced the deprivation of the Great Depression of the 1930s or World War II. Unlike the previous generation, young people at this time had fewer worries about obtaining such basics as food and shelter.

"I remember standing in some sweaty room and watching them on the stage, Keith and Brian—wow! I knew then that the Stones were great. They just had presence."[4]

– Ringo Starr, drummer for the Beatles

The Stones play to a packed audience in London in September 1963.

They were able instead to focus on issues including civil rights, women's rights, and their own personal freedoms. These freedoms included expanding definitions of what was and was not appropriate in regard to everything ranging from sexuality and drug use to music. For carefree young fans, there was nothing quite as exciting as a concert.

A DIFFERENT INVASION

The Rolling Stones recorded their second single, "I Wanna Be Your Man," in the fall of 1963. The song was written by John Lennon and Paul McCartney and later recorded by the Beatles. The Stones' version rose all the way to Number 12 on the UK singles chart. The band recorded a bluesy cover of the 1957 Buddy Holly hit "Not Fade Away" in early 1964, which likewise hit it big in Britain. The band then released it in the US market with "I Wanna Be Your Man" on the B side. It hit Number 48 on the *Billboard* Top 100 music chart.

Meanwhile, the music world was quickly taking note of what came to be known as the British Invasion, as British bands took over the American music charts. The British Invasion began with the Beatles. That band's *Meet the Beatles* record, released in the United States in January 1964, and its February appearance on the *Ed Sullivan Show* took the country by storm. The Beatles were followed by British bands including the Searchers, the Dave Clark Five, and in the summer of 1964, the Rolling Stones.

Singles vs. Albums

Long before music was shared in digital form, artists had a choice of releasing new songs individually as singles or waiting and releasing multiple songs together as an album. A single, released on a small vinyl record, actually came with two songs. The featured single was on the front, and there was another song on the back, called the B side. Artists might release a single to keep their name in front of the public while they worked on the full album that would include that song too, or they might release a single not tied to any album. The Rolling Stones had singles that did not appear on albums outside of later compilations, as well as albums with songs that were never released as singles. Initially, the band also released slightly different albums in Britain and the United States.

The British Invasion took over the American charts for roughly two years. Ironically, the music it featured had its roots in the blues, jazz, and R&B of African American artists such as Chuck Berry. Early American rock and roll artists such as Buddy Holly and Elvis Presley drew heavily from these beats for a new audience, but it took the British restyling of so-called race music to kick-start the rock and roll revolution.

Cereal Pitchmen

Like many bands, the Rolling Stones took on some unusual gigs as they worked to make a name for themselves. The band recorded a 26-second advertisement for Kellogg's Rice Krispies cereal in the early 1960s. It is believed that Jones wrote the jingle, which featured Jagger singing, "Wake up in the morning, there's a snap around the place."[5] The spot was not the only tie the group had to the advertising industry. Richards had interviewed for a job in advertising before joining the Stones, and Watts briefly worked for an advertising firm while building his drumming career.

CHAPTER FOUR

Albums, Tours, and Ed Sullivan

Decca released the Rolling Stones' first album on April 16, 1964. The band recorded the 12 songs on the album in just five days. This quick turnaround was possible in part because only one of the songs was an original. The rest were covers of popular R&B songs, so the recording sessions were handled much like gigs without the audience. In Britain, the album hit stores as *The Rolling Stones* and quickly climbed to the Number 1 spot. It was released in the United States in May with a few changes, retitled as *The Rolling Stones: England's Newest Hit Makers.* It began climbing the US charts as well and topped out at Number 11.

The Rolling Stones drew fans on Broadway in New York City for their tour in the summer of 1964.

TELEVISION
APPLIANCES
A SAUCY ROMP
THE PINK PANTHE

The debut album included the Motown hit "Can I Get a Witness." It also included a new song called "Tell Me." "Tell Me" was the first original song written by Jagger and Richards. The story goes that the two wrote it when Oldham locked them in his kitchen and would not let them out until they had a song. Unlike the other songs on the debut album, this one felt more reminiscent of the popular music of the time. Also released as a single in the United States, it became the band's first US Top 40 hit.

The Stones followed the album with the first of many US tours. Yet with the bulk of Stones fans in Britain, the tour barely registered in the states. It was not until the release of the band's second album, *12 X 5*, that things began to move. That album included a hit cover of "Time Is on My Side" and was released only in the United States. It paved the way for the same hit-making invitation that had rocketed the Beatles to stardom—a call to appear on the *Ed Sullivan Show*.

ED SULLIVAN

The *Ed Sullivan Show* was history's longest-running television variety program. It aired every Sunday evening on the CBS network from 1948 to 1971, hosted by journalist-turned-TV-host Ed Sullivan.

The show was known for the wide variety of acts it introduced to its television audience.

While everyone from comedians and actors to dancers and novelty acts had their time in the spotlight, Sullivan was especially important in introducing new musical acts to the American audience. Elvis Presley made his debut on the show in 1956, and Sullivan's 1964 Beatles show was among the most-watched television shows of the era.

The Rolling Stones made their first appearance on the *Ed Sullivan Show* on October 25, 1964. The band performed the Chuck Berry classic "Around and Around" to a chorus of screams from the audience. To Sullivan's dismay, the screams failed to end when the song did. The host had to urge the audience to be quiet and pay attention to the next act. The same thing happened again near the end of the show when the Stones closed it

Ed Sullivan and the Evolution of Music

Sullivan was among the first television hosts to introduce audiences to rock and roll in the late 1950s, featuring acts such as Elvis Presley. Following the launch of Motown Records in the early 1960s, Sullivan exposed his audiences to many of Motown's recording artists, including African American artists the Temptations, the Jackson 5, and the Supremes, among others. His promotion of such artists often resulted in complaints from both viewers and sponsors, but Sullivan refused to change. As a result, Americans of all races could see the talent, glamour, and grace of a variety of African American performers, helping to pave the way for the civil rights movement.

EBAL

Numerous TV appearances in 1964 brought the Stones new fans.

with the hit "Time Is on My Side." The noise was so loud after the music ended that no one could hear Sullivan's interview with Jagger.

The *Ed Sullivan Show* appearance was just what the Stones needed to ramp up their popularity with American audiences. As a result, the second US tour was far more successful than the first, and the band advanced Oldham's vision to make the Rolling Stones the opposite of the Beatles.

WOULD YOU WANT YOUR DAUGHTER TO MARRY A ROLLING STONE?

The Rolling Stones began as a blues band, with bandmates appearing on stage in suits, matching polished boots, and just slightly longer-than-average haircuts. As time went on and the band transitioned from blues and R&B covers to original music, its members evolved into the bad boys of rock and roll. Manager Oldham encouraged the transformation.

Even the first *Ed Sullivan Show* appearance brought its share of critics, with some viewers asking why Sullivan had allowed such "trash" on his stage.[1] The following year, the band played its first gig in Canada. Canadian Broadcasting Company journalist Larry Zolf asked the band directly about its bad-boy image. In an interview, he queried

They Did Marry Rolling Stones

Two Rolling Stones were already married when Canadian journalist Larry Zolf famously asked the band members, "Would you want your daughter to marry a Rolling Stone?"[4] Drummer Charlie Watts had married Shirley Shepherd in October 1964. Bassist Bill Wyman had married Diane Cory in 1959 (they divorced in 1969). Questions like this played down the band members' marriages and helped highlight the unmarried status of Jagger, Richards, and Jones to make the band more popular with female fans. Oldham shaped the whole band and especially Jagger as sex symbols.

them: would any of them let their daughter marry a Rolling Stone? A news item reviewing the Canadian concert featured the headline "Rolling Stones Show Violent and Vulgar."[2] That same year, Jagger, Richards, and Jones were fined five British pounds each (about $110 in US dollars in 2019) for urinating against the wall of a gas station in east London.[3]

By the end of 1965, the sex, drugs, and rock and roll reputation of the Stones was beginning to overtake the music. The band had moved on from covering popular blues songs to performing more original music. December 1964 had seen the release of the ballad "Heart of Stone" and "What a Shame"—both original songs penned by Jagger and Richards. True to form, the songs showcased the band's blues and R&B talents. The songs also marked the

The Stones intentionally projected a bad-boy image.

first time both sides of a Stones single featured original material.

In 1965, "The Last Time" became the first of the Stones' Number 1 hits in Britain that was written by Jagger and Richards. "The Last Time" was based on a 1955 gospel song, "This May Be the Last Time," made famous by the Staple Singers. The Staple Singers were an African American gospel, soul, and R&B group. Richards said turning an old gospel hit into a pop song led to a burst of confidence for himself and Jagger. At the same time, he said the song's success just meant they would be expected to create such new material again and again. When they pulled it off, the result changed the face of rock and roll forever.

"SATISFACTION" AT LAST

Shortly before the Stones' third American tour, the group's second tour as a main act, Richards made a discovery. He often kept a tape recorder by his bed so he could capture new songs when he thought of them. In spring 1965, he awoke to find that the tape in the recorder, which had been fresh the night before, was nearly at the end. He rewound and played the tape. He heard a three-note riff, his voice sleepily singing a simple lyric, and 40 minutes of snoring.

Jagger added the rest of the lyrics several days later. The band was on tour in Florida, where fans had rioted just four songs into the concert the night before. Band members fled from the

Bobby Womack and "It's All Over Now"

Like "The Last Time," the Stones hit "It's All Over Now" is a cover of a song from an African American group. The Valentinos first recorded the song, which was written by Bobby Womack and his sister-in-law Shirley Womack. Reportedly, Bobby Womack did not like the Stones' version of the song, though he did appreciate the royalties. He encouraged the band to do more of his songs and later worked with the Stones as a musician on the *Dirty Work* album. The song was the first Number 1 hit for the Stones in Britain.

riot and ended up hiding out at a nearby hotel. Legend has it Jagger took Richards's new tune and added lyrics while sitting by the hotel pool.

Richards said he had intended for the opening riff of "(I Can't Get No) Satisfaction" to be played by horns. However, there were no horns around when the Stones went into the studio to record the song less than a week after Jagger wrote the lyrics. Richards settled for using a foot pedal to add a buzzy tone to the guitar, thinking the recording was simply a dub and the horns would be added later. A dub is when an existing recording is copied to a

Nanker Phelge & the Glimmer Twins

A handful of Rolling Stones songs between 1963 and 1965 are credited to Nanker Phelge. Nanker Phelge was a pen name used for songs in which all Rolling Stones band members contributed to the songwriting. This let the band split the royalties.

The pen name comes from Jagger and Richards's former roommate Jimmy Phelge, combined with the British slang term *nanker*. A nanker is a goofy face someone makes by stretching his face with his hands.

Likewise, several Rolling Stones albums give production credits to the Glimmer Twins. According to Richards, this pen name came about in late 1968. Jagger and Richards were on a Brazilian cruise together with their girlfriends. Their fellow passengers recognized them and wanted more information on what the rock stars were doing. One of the passengers asked them to "Just give us a glimmer." Jagger quickly turned to Richards and announced "We're the Glimmer Twins."[5] The name stuck.

The Stones' first Number 1 hit has become an iconic rock song.

new recording, typically adding something else to it in the process.

Richards recalls being surprised when he heard "Satisfaction" on the radio. He said he had not even known that Oldham had released it. It quickly became the top song of the summer of 1965 and the Stones' first Number 1 hit in the United States.

The song's buzzy sound was new and captivating. In addition, Jagger's lyrics captured the sense of disconnection many young people were feeling between their longings and the realities of their consumer-driven society. The song also featured several sexually suggestive lyrics that upset some music producers and delighted many young fans.

"Satisfaction" marked the beginning of a new chapter for the Stones. This new era would be inseparable from the larger context of cultural change and social upheaval that occurred in the late 1960s and early 1970s. It would also change the face and the business of rock and roll for decades.

"What originally established the band was cover songs like 'Not Fade Away.' Then, later on, we got more well known ones like 'Satisfaction,' which you might say echoed the thinking of, well, any generation you care to name, including the present one. But we didn't set out on bits of paper that we were going to be the voice of a generation."[6]

– Mick Jagger, 1987

CHAPTER FIVE

Busted

By the end of 1965, the Rolling Stones had established themselves as a band to watch in the rapidly evolving genre of rock music. The following year saw Jagger and Richards penning a string of hits, including "Paint It, Black," "19th Nervous Breakdown," "Get Off My Cloud," and "Lady Jane." The 1966 album *Aftermath* was the Stones' first to feature all original material.

The group also began to branch out musically, despite a virtually nonstop touring schedule. Multi-instrumentalist Jones played the sitar on the Middle Eastern–themed "Paint It, Black," the marimba on "Under My Thumb," and the dulcimer and harpsichord

Jagger continued to perfect his exaggerated onstage moves, which were becoming legendary.

Richards, *front*, exemplified the rock star look as he headed to New York to appear on the *Ed Sullivan Show* in January 1967.

on "Lady Jane." "Let's Spend the Night Together" highlighted a piano, as opposed to the usual guitars. In the lyrics, Jagger further pushed the boundaries of songwriting, addressing prescription drug abuse in "Mother's Little Helper" and weaving sexual references into songs such as "Let's Spend the Night Together."

The Stones made a fifth appearance on the *Ed Sullivan Show* in January 1967. In an unusual move, the band accommodated requests from the show's producers to sing "Let's Spend the Night Together" as "Let's Spend Some Time Together" to be less suggestive.[1] Jagger rolled his eyes on camera when singing the altered line.

DRUG CHARGES

Like other bands of the time, the mid-1960s saw the Stones experimenting with what became known as psychedelic rock. The Beatles kicked off the trend in 1966 with the album *Revolver*, and the Stones followed suit in December 1967 with *Their Satanic Majesties Request*. The album was considered ambitious musically, though it quickly fell out of favor among fans.

However, it was the drugs behind the album that caused the most stir. By this time, the Stones were among a number of bands that were targeted

Psychedelic Rock

Psychedelic rock music draws its inspiration from hallucinogenic drugs such as LSD and magic mushrooms. The style uses feedback, electronics, and intense volume to recreate such experiences musically. The Grateful Dead was among the first rock bands to popularize the style, which originated on the US West Coast. Many other bands went on to experiment with the form, including such famous acts as the Doors and Jefferson Airplane. The style was not popular for long, but it influenced everything from fashion to poster art and also contributed to the development of heavy metal music.

by law enforcement for violating drug laws. The situation came to a head on February 12, 1967, at the home Richards had purchased in Sussex, England. Nearly 20 police officers raided the home just as Richards, Jagger, and several others were coming down from an LSD high. Richards and Jagger were arrested and taken to jail.

Soon after the bust, Oldham left Britain for the United States. In his place, American businessman Allen Klein bailed Richards and Jagger out of jail. Klein had begun working with the band in 1965 and had successfully negotiated improved contract terms with Decca. He now advised the band to leave the country until things quieted down.

The Stones soon left for Morocco, returning so Richards and Jagger could plead not guilty in court on May 10. They chose to take their case to trial, but they lost and subsequently were sentenced on June 29, 1967. Richards was found guilty and sentenced to 12 months in prison. Jagger likewise was found guilty, and he was sentenced to three months.

CRACKS IN THE STONES

The sentences sent shock waves through the music community. In support, the Who quickly recorded covers of "The Last Time" and "Under My Thumb." The Who proclaimed they did so to keep the work of the Stones in the public eye until Richards and Jagger were free to record once again. Meanwhile, an editor at the *Times of London* publicly criticized the case as a setup. As a conservative newspaper, the *Times* generally opposed the use of illegal drugs. The fact that the paper ran the editorial virtually confirmed that the musicians were being unfairly targeted. A storm of protest ensued over the convictions, and each man ultimately spent less than a week in jail.

In the meantime, Jones had also had a brush with the law over drugs. Police raided his London apartment in early May 1967, catching him and some friends using marijuana. This time, the press had been alerted to the upcoming bust and arrived even before the police. Jones was given a warning,

Jones parties with actress Anita Pallenberg at the Cannes Film Festival in May 1967, as his drug use was getting out of control.

but he was arrested once again a year later as his drug habit continued to intensify.

It also was around this time that Jones became increasingly estranged from the rest of the band. Richards remembers becoming accustomed to

performing without Jones, even on tour. He began missing recording sessions as well, leaving the other band members scrambling to find the right sound when they were short one musician. Jones's drug issues also raised questions about whether he would be able to get the visas needed to tour with the band outside of the United Kingdom.

In his autobiography, Richards says he believes it was hard for Jones to accept that Jagger and Richards were now in essence the band leaders due to their songwriting. The evolving sounds of the band also were taking it farther and farther from its blues roots. But it was the blues that was most important to Jones as a musician. Jones contributed to 1968's *Beggars Banquet*, an album counted among the best the Stones ever produced. His blues slide guitar work on "No Expectations" remains among the best examples of the genre.

Jones left the Rolling Stones in early 1969 to explore solo projects. The band officially fired Jones from the Stones in June 1969 and replaced him with

Mick Taylor

Michael Kevin Taylor was born on January 17, 1949, in Welwyn Garden City, England. He began playing guitar at age nine, taught by his uncle. As a child, he saw a concert by rockers Bill Haley and the Comets, which inspired his musical explorations. Taylor played in several bands as a teenager, then had a last-minute opportunity in 1965 to take the place of world-famous guitarist Eric Clapton when he failed to show up for a gig with John Mayall's Bluesbreakers. It was Mayall who recommended Taylor to Jagger as Jones's replacement. Taylor played his first gig with the Stones on July 5, 1969. He is widely regarded as the best technical guitarist to work with the group due to his skill with many guitar-playing techniques.

guitarist Mick Taylor. Despite his many talents and accomplishments, Jones remained dogged by drug and alcohol addictions. He was found drowned in the swimming pool of his Sussex home in July 1969 at age 27.

SOUNDS OF THE TIMES

Just as the late 1960s were marked by the antiestablishment counterculture, so too were they marked by conflict. The civil rights movement and the United States' role in the Vietnam War (1954–1975) had Americans of all ages and backgrounds marching in the streets. The Stones' *Beggars Banquet* was both a response to the times and an important redirection of the band's musical focus from the psychedelic style of *Satanic Majesties* to something more aligned with its blues roots.

Songs such as "Street Fighting Man," "Sympathy

> "The band weren't really worried about replacing Brian [Jones] because in '68–69 they were top of the heap. They could have had anybody they wanted, including God himself. [Renowned guitarist Eric] Clapton came to a recording session. Mick Taylor was very quiet and shy, but they got him playing. He was right. He could play."[2]
>
> *– Ian Stewart*

Responses to the violence and devastation of the Vietnam War included mass demonstrations and work from artists like the Rolling Stones.

for the Devil," and "Gimme Shelter" captured the tumult of the era. In the minds of many, the counterculture had failed and it was now everyone for himself or herself. By the time the Stones began their fifth US tour in November 1969, the Beatles had broken up, Taylor had integrated into the band, and the Stones were filling coliseums and stadiums. Mid-1969 hits such as "Jumpin' Jack Flash" and "Honky Tonk Women" helped the band regain the momentum it had lost with *Satanic Majesties*.

The band had played more than 20 shows in two months and planned to conclude its tour with one last stop. The Altamont Speedway Free Concert was supposed to be the West Coast's answer to the legendary Woodstock music festival that had taken place earlier that year in New York State. It was a star-studded lineup intended to close out the summer of 1969, called the Summer of Love, and the 1960s in general.

The event turned tragic during the Rolling Stones' set, which came at the end of the concert. The Stones had hired the Hells Angels motorcycle gang to provide security, something the band was encouraged to do by rock band the Grateful Dead. However, the Hells Angels gang in the United States was considerably more violent

Merry Clayton & "Gimme Shelter"

The stunning and haunting background vocals that transformed "Gimme Shelter" were a late addition. The Stones were in a recording session with a new American producer, Jimmy Miller, when he said something was missing. Longtime Stones collaborator Jack Nitzsche suggested adding a vocal layer featuring Merry Clayton, who had sung with Ray Charles, Elvis Presley, and other famous artists.

Clayton was 20 years old, pregnant, and in her pajamas and hair rollers when the late-night call came to report to the studio. Her husband, jazz saxophonist Curtis Amy, convinced her to go. "Gimme Shelter" became the most praised of all the Rolling Stones songs that weren't released as singles.

The Stones beginning their set at Altamont, shortly before the deadly scuffle

than the Hells Angels gang in the United Kingdom. A scuffle broke out in front of the stage during the Stones' set, and a young fan was stabbed to death by the motorcycle gang. The entire event was

captured on film in the rock documentary *Gimme Shelter*. The tragedy left the members of the Stones shaken and shocked, and they left the country the following day.

CHAPTER SIX

Commercial Success

Just days before the tragedy at the Altamont Free Concert, the Rolling Stones released their eighth album. *Let It Bleed* charted at Number 1 in the United Kingdom and Number 3 in the United States. It is best known for two songs: "Gimme Shelter" and "You Can't Always Get What You Want." Like 1968's *Beggars Banquet*, *Let It Bleed* demonstrated a return to American roots music, this time including gospel.

The Rolling Stones introduced new guitarist Mick Taylor, *second from left*, in 1969.

Even before the album's release, the Stones had begun work on their next project. The band began recording the album *Sticky Fingers* in 1969, though it would not be released until 1971. It was the first full album to feature Taylor on guitar and included the hits "Brown Sugar," "Can't You Hear Me Knocking," and "Wild Horses." The album also featured a now-iconic design created by artist Andy Warhol. The art features a close-up of a man's pants with a zipper that actually works. It was like the Rolling Stones' members themselves: racy, bold, and a bit coarse.

The Rolling Stones Logo

Few bands had their own logo when Jagger approached London's Royal College of Art in 1969. He was seeking a student to create artwork for an upcoming album. Jagger hired 24-year-old John Pasche to design the iconic Hot Lips logo for £50, about $1,000 in US dollars in 2019.[1]

Jagger originally wanted artwork of Kali, the Hindu goddess of energy. Many representations of Kali do feature the goddess with her tongue out. However, Pasche said the idea for the Hot Lips logo came to him as soon as he noticed Jagger's lips and mouth. The logo first was used on *Sticky Fingers*.

In February 1970, band members received a double dose of bad news. They learned that their manager (Allen Klein), not the band, owned the recording rights and masters of their songs. They also learned that no one had been paying

The Stones returned to the Marquee Club in London for a farewell performance in March 1971.

taxes on their earnings for the past seven years. "I discovered nothing had been paid and I owed a fortune," Jagger recalled.[2] Later that year, they cut their ties to Klein and Decca Records and began to form their own label, Rolling Stones Records, in conjunction with Atlantic Records.

Without the money to pay their taxes, the Stones exiled themselves to France. The musicians had just completed their European tour and released a live album. Now, they, their family members, and other key musicians and technicians left Britain to set up a new recording base in a rented house in Nice, France.

EXILED

The summer of 1971 saw the Stones putting together what would become one of their most highly regarded albums. It was recorded in a basement, with the Stones' mobile recording truck parked outside. Jagger was living in Paris. Watts was living three hours away. Richards ended up leading the haphazard album process, with the tracks put down during all-night recording sessions. One exception is "Happy," which Richards recorded one early morning. He came to the makeshift studio only to find the other Stones were not there. Instead, Richards recruited producer Jimmy Miller to play the drums. He pulled in Bobby Keys, who

Keith, Mick, and the Cut-Up

The Rolling Stones tapped many sources of creative energy to create the acclaimed album *Exile on Main Street*. One of those techniques was borrowed from novelist William Burroughs, author of *Naked Lunch*. To use this cut-up method, the writer chooses random words and phrases cut from printed sentences and then randomly reassembles these words and phrases to inspire a new sentence or, in this case, lyric. "Casino Boogie" was written in this way.

was at that time playing with the Stones, to play the baritone saxophone. Richards sang the song, and the remaining instruments were laid over the track later.

Exile on Main Street hit record stores in May 1972. Reviewers called the double album a dense tangle of sound, with only the occasional voice or instrument breaking through. That included Jagger, whose garbled voice becomes virtually just another instrument. Yet the critically acclaimed music hid an uglier reality of personal problems within and among the band members. Richards and his longtime partner, Anita Pallenberg—formerly Jones's girlfriend—had become heavy drug users. Visitors to the house in France recall seeing heroin, cocaine, and marijuana, along with a steady stream of drug dealers and party-goers.

The activity caught the eye of local authorities, who arrested Richards and Pallenberg and charged them with possession of heroin and intent to traffic. The two were found guilty and banned from entering France for two years, prohibiting the Stones from touring there. The two left France in November 1971, and the band wrapped up *Exile on Main Street* at a studio in Los Angeles, California. In early 1972, Richards entered treatment for drug addiction.

The 1972 North American Tour

The Stones recovered from Altamont with their 1972 North American tour. The tour took along the largest entourage up to that point in concert history, featuring a doctor and a press corps that included photographer Annie Leibovitz and writer Truman Capote. Despite the operation's size, tickets were available for $6.50 each, which was about $40 in 2019.[4] The opening act was 22-year-old Stevie Wonder, who was in the process of becoming a musical legend himself.

The 1972 tour featured a staggering 48 shows in 54 days. As Richards recalls, there were no formal guidelines for the shows. "You sort of made it up and you went along," he said.[5] This unique flexibility became a fixture for the Stones. While most bands agree in advance on who is playing what, the Stones have been known to improvise. They never quite play the same concert twice. In 2017, the 1972 tour earned a place on *Rolling Stone* magazine's list of the 50 Greatest Concerts of the Last 50 Years.

The next eight years saw the Stones release five more hit albums. *Goats Head Soup*, released in 1973, featured the hit ballad "Angie." *It's Only Rock 'n' Roll*, released in 1974, recorded a hit with its title track. *Black and Blue*, featuring "Fool to Cry," came out in 1976. While the album hit Number 1 for four weeks, one critic referred to the work as the "first meaningless Rolling Stones album."[3] It contained a mix of funk, reggae, and soul, but none of the guitar-heavy rock and roll that fans desired.

OLD PROBLEMS, NEW MEMBERS

While the 1970s were musically productive

for the Rolling Stones, the band's extensive touring schedule, contract disputes, creative differences, and drug issues took a toll on the individual members. At one point, band members avoided both France and Britain due to tax issues. Drug arrests in the two countries also forced them to schedule around those areas during European tours.

Richards in particular continued to battle drug addiction. Police raided his London residence in 1973 and confiscated marijuana, heroin, a handgun, and a rifle, among other things. In 1977, Canadian police found heroin in Richards's hotel room. He was due to go to prison for up to seven years when a blind woman stepped forward to tell how Richards had helped secure her safety at Stones concerts. The judge in the case suspended the sentence and ordered Richards to play a benefit concert for the Canadian National Institute for the Blind. Richards eventually gave up heroin in 1978.

Tensions among band members also escalated during the 1970s. Richards's and Jagger's drug charges limited where the band could tour, and they were unable to perform in Japan as a result. No longer tethered to homes in the United Kingdom, the band members scattered among several countries. Jagger, now married, spent more and more time away from the band. That left

Ronnie Wood, *left*, onstage with Mick Jagger

Richards to do more of the work on the music. At the same time, drug use eroded the contributions of not only Richards but also producer Jimmy Miller, who left the band after *Goats Head Soup*. In late 1974, Taylor quit the band, saying he did not feel his songwriting contributions were being acknowledged.

Taylor's departure left the Stones without a rhythm guitarist. The members auditioned several musicians, including guitarists Peter Frampton and Jeff Beck. Beck, like Eric Clapton, had played with the Yardbirds. Eventually, they settled on Ronnie Wood of the band the Faces.

Wood, who had known the Rolling Stones band members since the mid-1960s, had been a session collaborator with the Stones in 1973 on "It's Only Rock 'n' Roll (But I Like It)." Wood's new role with the band was announced in April 1975, and he joined in as the Stones kicked off their Tour of the Americas in May 1975.

NEW FANS WITH *SOME GIRLS*

The second half of the 1970s ushered in new sounds in pop music. The aggressive, rebellious version of rock known as punk took root in both Britain and the United States through groups such as the Sex Pistols and the Ramones. At the same time, the beat-driven sounds of disco bubbled out beyond dance clubs and onto the airwaves. The disco trend was driven by acts including the Bee Gees, Gloria Gaynor, and K. C. and the Sunshine Band.

Yet the Stones soon proved they were far bigger than any personal problems or changes

> "The Beatles remained innocent but the Rolling Stones didn't. The Stones used dark elements in a very savage way. The rhythms were much more ferocious and their vocal techniques were much more violent. Of course, it all had the might of decibels behind it."[6]
>
> *– Wilfrid Mellers, musicologist*

in musical taste. *Some Girls* hit the charts in 1978. The album was hailed as the group's best since *Exile on Main Street*. As with prior Stones work, the album not only mined traditional veins of country music, blues, and rock and roll but also cashed in on both the punk and disco crazes with hits like "Miss You" and "Beast of Burden." The disco-inspired "Miss You" hit Number 1 on the *Billboard* Hot 100. *Some Girls* captured new fans for the band while reminding others why they stayed loyal in the first place.

CHAPTER SEVEN

Live in Concert!

In 1979, the now-revitalized Rolling Stones headed back to the studio, this time in the Bahamas, to continue work on their next album. As Richards recalls, "There were ripples of arguments between Mick and me that would grow into a rumble soon."[1] Richards acknowledged that his struggles with drug use in the 1970s had forced Jagger to take on the lion's share of work in the studio. Now free of his heroin addiction, Richards wanted more input. He recalls that Jagger did not always appreciate that.

The early 1980s was a successful time for the Stones. *From left*: Charlie Watts, Keith Richards, Bill Wyman, Mick Jagger, and Ronnie Wood

The Stones released *Emotional Rescue* in June 1980. It was the band's seventeenth US studio album and featured the hits "She's So Cold" and the title track. Despite lukewarm reviews, the album sold well in both the United States and Britain. The song "Emotional Rescue" went on to hit Number 3 on the *Billboard* Hot 100. The album did not, however, spur a tour. That was saved for the Stones' next effort, *Tattoo You*, released in August 1981.

"Mick needs to know what he's going to do tomorrow. Me, I'm just happy to wake up and see who's hanging around. Mick's rock, I'm roll."[2]

– *Keith Richards*

Many music critics regard *Tattoo You* as the Rolling Stones' last great album. The record included many songs that had been rolling around unfinished for years. Even the hit "Start Me Up" had been in the works since 1975. For many fans, *Tattoo You* marked a return to the Stones' most creative work. *Tattoo You* welcomed listeners back with bluesy tales of love lost, killer saxophone parts courtesy of Sonny Rollins, and a very human admission that, yes, even the Stones were getting older.

Tattoo You also represented a sea change in how the Rolling Stones approached the music business. US concerts were booked almost exclusively in large arenas and stadiums. Sometimes the band performed multiple concerts in the same city. Nearly three million people had seen the band perform by the time the 50-date *Tattoo You* tour ended in December 1981.[3]

Reggae Roots

"Start Me Up" is a classic rock song that began as a reggae song. Richards started putting together the song while the band was compiling its *Black and Blue* album in 1975. He recalls doing nearly 50 takes, but the song never quite worked. The Stones took the song up again when recording *Some Girls*. This time, Richards played it as a rock song. Producer Chris Kimsey recalls that Richards didn't like that version, so he asked that it be erased. Kimsey didn't trash it, however, and the song became the top single on *Tattoo You* three years later.

MAKING MONEY

Over the next two decades, the Rolling Stones would shift from a focus on chart-topping albums to a focus on live performances. The 1981 tour in support of *Tattoo You* set a new record for earnings. In addition to an estimated $34 million from ticket sales, tour merchandise sales averaged $10 per purchaser, or close to $20 million. The Stones also arranged a cable television pay-per-view option for selected shows at a cost of $10 per subscriber. Finally, fragrance maker Jovan, Inc. signed on to the tour as a sponsor for several million dollars.[4]

Mick Jagger and the Stones appeared before a packed crowd at Wembley Stadium in London as part of their 1982 tour of Europe.

The Stones also successfully took the *Tattoo You* tour to Europe. It was the first time in six years the band had toured on that continent. The members also signed a new recording contract with CBS. At $50 million, it was the biggest recording contract ever at that point in time.[5]

The 1983 album *Undercover* was the band's last for Atlantic Records. It made it to Number 4

on the US chart, but no higher. Meanwhile, the band was coming closer than ever to breaking up. Long-simmering tensions between Jagger and Richards reached a boiling point when Jagger turned his focus to his solo albums: 1985's *She's the Boss* and 1987's *Primitive Cool*. His attention to those projects forced Richards and Ronnie Wood to do the heavy lifting on 1986's *Dirty Work*.

Dirty Work failed to satisfy critics, who had been hoping for a better effort from such a successful band. In addition, the band lost longtime road manager and former Stone Ian Stewart to a heart attack in 1985.

The next few years saw a scattered band embarking on a variety of independent projects. Watts performed with his Charlie Watts Orchestra around England and Germany. Wyman had become involved in charity performances with a project known as Willie and the Poor Boys. Wood continued working on solo albums, collaborations, and his own artwork.

Like Jagger, Richards released a solo album and toured with his own band, the X-Pensive Winos. Richards said the experience gave him a new appreciation for Jagger's role with the Stones. "You realize that you're it all the time," he said of being the front man. "I have choices. The front man has no choice."[6]

WHEELS TURNING AGAIN

Richards credits the band's time off in the late 1980s for its resurgent work, *Steel Wheels*, released in 1989. Wood, who helped bring Jagger and Richards back together for a creative meeting, said the time apart also helped them see the value of being together. Some fans even argued that one of the hits on *Steel Wheels*, "Mixed Emotions," was more of a commentary on the Jagger-Richards relationship than anything else.

The *Steel Wheels* tour kicked off in August 1989—seven years after the band's last tour dates for *Tattoo You*. As with that tour, the *Steel Wheels* tour was a spectacle, played to huge audiences in the largest venues. The events also featured touring vocalists and a keyboardist. The band followed the *Steel Wheels* tour in the United States with ten shows in Japan. It then changed sets and kicked off the Urban Jungle tour in Europe.

Wyman recalls the challenges of playing 120

The Rolling Stones on Film

The Rolling Stones have been the subject of a number of documentaries over the years. *Charlie Is My Darling* was released in 1966 and features two days in the life of the band during the 1965 Ireland tour. In 1969, *Stones in the Park* captured the band's July 5 concert in London's Hyde Park. The event happened just two days after Brian Jones's tragic death. Similarly, 1970's *Gimme Shelter* captured the tragic death of a fan at the Altamont Speedway Free Concert.

Released in 1996, *The Rolling Stones Rock and Roll Circus* was originally conceived as a television special when it was filmed in 1968. Release of the film was delayed because the band members were concerned that the Who, one of multiple acts in the film, had given a better performance than the Stones.

More recently, 2008's *Shine a Light* featured footage from the *A Bigger Bang* tour. In 2010, *Stones in Exile* documented the creation of the landmark *Exile on Main Street* album. In 2012, the documentary *Crossfire Hurricane* paid homage to 50 years of the Stones.

Sharing the Stage

The Rolling Stones have hosted a wide range of musical guests in their many years on stage. From opening acts to shared bills, the band has embraced a wide variety of artists, including its own blues heroes as well as rockers, rappers, and country singers. Featured blues and R&B performers have included Chuck Berry, Ike and Tina Turner, Etta James, and John Lee Hooker. Notable rock acts included the Who, the Yardbirds, Alice Cooper, Journey, and Maroon 5. Individual artists who've appeared with the band include famed guitarist Prince, former Yardbirds guitarists Eric Clapton and Jeff Beck, Pete Townshend of the Who, folk legend Bob Dylan, rapper Kanye West, and singer-songwriter Janis Joplin.

gigs before more than seven million people during these three major tours. He decided to retire at the end. "I was happy to move on because there were so many other things that I wanted to do in my life," he said.[7] After a lengthy search, the Stones replaced Wyman with bassist Darryl Jones in 1993. Jones, a Chicago native, played with jazz great Miles Davis early in his career.

Jones's first album with the Stones was 1994's *Voodoo Lounge*. The album was heralded as a return to classic Stones music, featuring bar-pumping rock, solid R&B, and Jagger's voice alternating between predatory slurs and heartbreaking confessions. It was something fans hadn't heard since *Tattoo You* in 1981, and it showed that the Stones were still willing to challenge themselves musically.

Darryl Jones, *right*, joined the Stones on the *Voodoo Lounge* tour.

The *Voodoo Lounge* world tour kicked off in August 1994 and rolled through 117 dates on six continents.

At the time, it was yet again rock's most successful tour, as well as one of the most expensive. It took some 450 employees per venue to make the event happen. In return, fans shelled out more than $50 per ticket. The full tour took in an estimated $300 million, another record at that time.[8]

By early 1995, the tour had not even wrapped when *Voodoo Lounge* won the Grammy Award for

Best Rock Album. The "Love Is Strong" video also won for Best Music Video—Short Form. While the band had been nominated for multiple Grammy Awards in the past, these honors were the first time it actually won.

Two years later, the Stones were back on the road again to promote their 1997 album *Bridges to Babylon*. The tour went on to become the second-highest-grossing rock tour at the time, second only to the *Voodoo Lounge* tour. Meanwhile, critics labeled *Bridges to Babylon* a failed attempt at modernizing the Stones' sound for the techno-heavy 1990s. The band followed *Bridges* with the No Security tour in 1999 and the Licks tour in 2002–2003.

In 2005, the band released another album of new material, *A Bigger Bang*. Once again, the release defied critics and delighted fans, with many seeing in this work a return to the band's treasured blues roots. Richards credits some of this to the forced circumstances under which he and Jagger had to work. Beginning with *Exile on Main Street*, the band had for years contributed to songs from distant locations. *A Bigger Bang* began in the same way. Then Watts was diagnosed with throat cancer. As Richards recalls, he and Jagger realized they soon might be the only two original band members left. They continued their work, keeping the tracks intentionally simple and spare. Watts eventually recovered and helped finish the album. Yet the experience had left its mark. "There's no hiding place if there's only three of you in the room," Jagger said.[9]

The Stones supported *A Bigger Bang* with a two-year, 144-show mega tour that boasted more than $500 million in revenue. Attendance at the shows totaled 4.68 million.[10] The Stones were first introduced as the greatest rock and roll band in the world in July 1969. Nearly 40 years later, *A Bigger Bang* continued to prove it.

Millions of Fans in One Place

The Rolling Stones' free concert on February 18, 2006, on Copacabana Beach in Rio de Janeiro, Brazil, ranks among the largest concerts of all time. The show, part of the *A Bigger Bang* tour, required a stage the height of a seven-story building. Attendance was estimated at 1.5 million people.[11]

Despite the giant crowd, the Stones do not hold the record for largest-ever concert. While that also took place at Copacabana Beach, the artist was Rod Stewart in 1994. Estimated attendance at his free concert was 3.5 million, although there is some question about whether the area could even accommodate that many fans.[12]

CHAPTER EIGHT

The World's Greatest Rock Band

More than 50 years after the Rolling Stones began performing, the band continues to sell out the world's largest stadiums. The core musical group—Jagger, Richards, and Watts—represents the longest-lasting partnership in the history of rock music.

The band's success has not been without challenges. The Stones have persevered through changes in the lineup, squabbles among members, drug addictions, and changing trends in musical tastes. In 1986, the band received a Grammy Award for Lifetime Achievement. Three years later,

Jagger speaks at the Stones' induction into the Rock & Roll Hall of Fame.

the Stones were inducted into the Rock & Roll Hall of Fame.

In the summer of 2012, Jagger, Richards, Watts, and Wood returned to the site of the old Marquee Club for a photo. The photo marked the fiftieth anniversary of their first gig. Jagger told *Rolling Stone* magazine he felt they were cheating just a bit because Watts and Woods had not been a part of the original band.

Jagger also said he never imagined the band would stay together as long as it had. "Groups in those days and singers didn't really last very long," he said.[1] He noted that even Elvis Presley had only lasted about ten years.

Playing a Pirate

In 2007, Richards was recruited to play the father of Johnny Depp's Captain Jack Sparrow character in the Pirates of the Caribbean movie franchise. Richards said he never expected to be in a Disney movie. However, the longtime friend of actor Depp said his two cameos in the Pirates of the Caribbean franchise were a good experience. Playing a pirate meant he had to wake up slightly earlier than usual, he said, but other things were familiar. "I've been looting and pillaging all my life," he joked. "It was just the costume was heavier."[2] He said he enjoyed the chance to introduce more young people to rock and roll. He also didn't mind if they referred to him not as Keith Richards but rather as Jack Sparrow's dad.

NO FILTER, NO STOPPING

One of the hallmarks of the Stones' career is the way the band has broken barriers.

It has introduced a variety of musical styles to new audiences. It has changed audience expectations of what a live concert can be. And it has taken US-born rock and roll to audiences around the world. In March 2016, the band broke yet another barrier, becoming the first major international rock band to play in Cuba. The free concert drew more than 100,000 fans.[3] Rock music had been banned on Cuban TV and radio since the Cuban Revolution in the 1950s.

In December 2016, the band returned to its roots with *Blue & Lonesome*, an album of covers. The album went on to capture the Grammy Award for Best Traditional Blues Album. In September 2017, the Stones kicked off the European leg of their No Filter tour.

No Filter came to the United States in June 2019, with a sold-out performance at Soldier Field in Chicago, Illinois. The tour had

Blue & Lonesome

It was American blues that brought Jones, Jagger, and Richards together to form the Rolling Stones. What may be surprising is how long it took the group to record a blues-only album. That finally happened in December 2015 when the Stones recorded *Blue & Lonesome*. The pure blues album was the band's first all-covers studio release since 1964's *The Rolling Stones*. It was recorded over a three-day period in a studio just down the street from the site of the Crawdaddy Club, where the band was in residence in early 1963.

The Stones drew huge crowds at their 2016 concert in Cuba.

been delayed slightly due to Jagger's health. The 75-year-old singer had undergone surgery in April 2019 to replace a heart valve. Yet just one month after the surgery, Jagger posted a video on Twitter showing himself rehearsing his famous dance moves.

Like the *A Bigger Bang* tour, the No Filter tour set new records in the music industry. The three-leg, three-year tour grossed more than $415 million.[4] That made it the eighth-highest-grossing tour of all time. It also made the Rolling Stones the only band with two of the top-ten highest grossing concert tours of all time.

Moves Like Jagger

In 2011, the American pop band Maroon 5 had a hit with "Moves Like Jagger." The song was a nod to the famous dance moves of the Rolling Stones front man. Pop artists Kesha and Michelle Branch likewise have mentioned Jagger or the Stones in their lyrics.

Jagger's onstage moves are legendary even as he continues to front the Stones in his 70s, into the 2020s. Jagger credits this success to a lifetime of training with a focus on maintaining stamina. He says he works out five to six times per week by running, swimming, kickboxing, and cycling. However, he says the secret to maintaining his balance while on stage is frequent ballet practice.

INFLUENCING OTHER ARTISTS

The Rolling Stones have had an outsized impact on the work of other artists. While many artists count

The Stones were still putting on epic live shows in the summer of 2019.

the Stones among their musical influences, others are more direct in their references. Pearl Jam has frequently played covers of Rolling Stones songs in its concerts. Both Liz Phair and Jon Spencer put out albums designed as responses to the Stones' iconic *Exile on Main Street*. Megastar Bruce Springsteen called the "Street Fighting Man" lyric "What can a poor boy do except to sing for a rock and roll band" one of the greatest rock and roll lines of all time.[5] The influence of the Stones' style also is clear in the music of rock bands from Aerosmith to the White Stripes. The Rolling Stones are the original bad boys of rock and roll.

"What Muddy Waters did for us is what we should do for others," Keith Richards said. "It's the old thing, what you want written on your tombstone as a musician: 'He passed it on.'"[6]

Music critics also point to the band's willingness to take risks onstage. Many artists carefully script their live performances, laying out what they play and who plays it. The Stones are willing to improvise on stage based on what they think their audience wants to hear that day.

Likewise, the Rolling Stones had a profound influence on Western culture. The band was rarely hesitant about pushing the boundaries of what was accepted in polite society. The original album cover for *Beggars Banquet* in 1968 featured a photo of a

The musical and cultural legacy of the Rolling Stones will last for many generations.

dirty toilet and a graffiti-covered wall. It was banned until the 1980s. The hit "Brown Sugar" touched upon slavery, rape, interracial sex, and drugs, among other topics that were taboo at the time. "All the nasty subjects in one go," Jagger said of the song in a 1995 interview. "I never would write that song now."[7]

LIVING LEGENDS

The Rolling Stones were among a handful of bands that took part in the British Invasion of the US music scene in the mid-1960s. They are the only one of those bands still enjoying commercially successful tours.

Music industry analysts credit the band's unusual longevity to its willingness to put the group ahead of any individual egos. The Stones' members also have proved themselves to be smart businesspeople. Maintaining a tour schedule even into their seventies has allowed them to continue filling stadiums. With more than 400 songs, two dozen studio albums, ten mega tours, and more than 200 million records sold, the Rolling Stones have written their own page in the history of music.[8]

"We'll die on stage, I suppose. What a way to go."[9]

– Ronnie Wood

TIMELINE

1938
Ian Stewart is born on July 18.

1941
Charlie Watts is born on June 2.

1942
Brian Jones is born on February 28.

1943
Mick Jagger is born on July 26; Keith Richards is born on December 18.

1961
Jagger and Richards reconnect after many years when they meet again on a train station platform.

1962
In July, Mick Jagger and the Rollin' Stones play their first gig at London's Marquee Club.

1964
In October, the Rolling Stones make their first appearance on the *Ed Sullivan Show*.

1965
"(I Can't Get No) Satisfaction" hits Number 1 in the United States.

1969
The Rolling Stones part ways with Brian Jones in June; Jones is found dead less than a month later, and Mick Taylor is named as his replacement.

1971
In April, the Rolling Stones release *Sticky Fingers*, the first of eight consecutive Number 1 albums in the United States.

1972
In May, the Stones release their landmark *Exile on Main Street* album after recording it in France during the band's tax exile.

1974
Taylor leaves the band in December and is replaced by Ronnie Wood in 1975.

1978

"Miss You" hits Number 1 in the United States, ending a nearly five-year drought of hits.

1981

In August, *Tattoo You* is released; it is considered by many to be the last great album from the band.

1985

Band founder Ian Stewart dies of a heart attack.

1989

The Rolling Stones are inducted into the Rock & Roll Hall of Fame.

1993

Bill Wyman leaves the band and is replaced by Darryl Jones.

1995

Voodoo Lounge wins the band's first Grammy Award for Best Rock Album.

2005

In August, the Rolling Stones kick off the *A Bigger Bang* tour.

2016

Blue & Lonesome, the band's first studio album in 20 years, is released and wins the Grammy Award for Best Traditional Blues Album.

2019

The Rolling Stones kick off the US leg of the No Filter tour in Chicago in June following Jagger's heart surgery.

ESSENTIAL FACTS

Rolling Stones Band Members

- **Mick Jagger** provides lead and backing vocals and plays rhythm guitar.
- **Keith Richards** plays lead, rhythm, and bass guitar and sings backing and some lead vocals.
- **Charlie Watts** has played drums for the Stones since January 1963.
- **Bill Wyman** was the Stones' bass player from December 1962 until January 1993.
- **Brian Jones** was the band's cofounder, along with pianist Ian Stewart. He left the band in 1969.
- **Ian Stewart** cofounded the band with Jones in 1962, but he was removed from the official lineup in 1963.
- **Mick Taylor** replaced Brian Jones in 1969 and played guitar and sang backing vocals until 1974.
- **Ronnie Wood** plays lead, rhythm, and bass guitar and sings backing vocals. He joined the band in 1975.
- **Darryl Jones** took over bass from Bill Wyman in 1993. He also sings backing vocals.

Rolling Stones Studio Albums

- *The Rolling Stones* (1964)
- *12 X 5* (1964)
- *The Rolling Stones No. 2/The Rolling Stones, Now!* (1965)
- *Out of Our Heads* (1965)
- *December's Children (And Everybody Else's)* (1965)
- *Aftermath* (1966)
- *Between the Buttons* (1967)
- *Their Satanic Majesties Request* (1967)
- *Beggars Banquet* (1968)
- *Let It Bleed* (1969)
- *Sticky Fingers* (1971)
- *Exile on Main Street* (1972)
- *Goats Head Soup* (1973)
- *It's Only Rock 'n' Roll (But I Like It)* (1974)

- *Black and Blue* (1976)
- *Some Girls* (1978)
- *Emotional Rescue* (1980)
- *Tattoo You* (1981)
- *Undercover* (1983)
- *Dirty Work* (1986)
- *Steel Wheels* (1989)
- *Voodoo Lounge* (1994)
- *Bridges to Babylon* (1997)
- *A Bigger Bang* (2005)
- *Blue & Lonesome* (2016)

Career Highlights

The Rolling Stones have become one of music's longest-lasting acts. The Stones' combination of talent, drive, and a shared love of the traditionally African American sounds of the blues, R&B, and jazz helped bring these genres to millions of new fans around the world.

Conflicts

Tensions between band members Mick Jagger and Keith Richards are legend. Jagger's detail-oriented perfectionism often clashed with Richards's easygoing nature. Sometimes they argued over creative control. Other times they fought over the negative impacts of Richards's drug use or the threat of Jagger's solo career.

Quote

"We didn't set out on bits of paper that we were going to be the voice of a generation."

—Mick Jagger, 1987

GLOSSARY

cameo
A small but noticeable appearance of a celebrity in a film, play, song, or other art form.

catcall
A sound or noise that someone (such as an audience member) makes toward a performer that he or she does not like.

counterculture
A culture of values that go against those of established society, popularized in the 1960s.

cover
To record or perform a song that was previously recorded by someone else.

debut
The first appearance, often of an album or publication, made by a musician or group.

exile
A person who has been forced to live in a foreign country.

front man
The leader in a band, usually the singer.

gig
A job for a musician, actor, or other performer.

jazz
A genre of music developed by African Americans in New Orleans in the early 1900s.

LSD
An illegal drug that causes people to see and hear things that do not really exist.

moonlight
To work at a second job.

psychedelic
Influenced by the drug culture of hallucinations and altered perceptions.

R&B
Rhythm and blues; a type of pop music of African American origin that has a soulful vocal style that features improvisation.

riff
A short and usually repeated pattern of notes in a song.

royalties
A share of money generated by sales of a work.

skiffle
A kind of folk music with a blues or jazz influence, played by a small group, that often used improvised musical instruments, such as washboards.

taboo
Forbidden due to moral or social customs.

ADDITIONAL RESOURCES

Selected Bibliography

Richards, Keith, and James Fox. *Life*. Bay Back, 2011.

Turner, Steve. "The Rolling Stones: A Career in Quotes." *Guardian*, 26 Jan. 2013, theguardian.com. Accessed 2 Jan. 2020.

Further Readings

Cummings, Judy Dodge. *The Beatles*. Abdo, 2022.

Moore, Shannon Baker. *A History of Music*. Abdo, 2015.

Turn It Up! A Pitch-Perfect History of Music That Rocked the World. National Geographic Kids, 2019.

Online Resources

To learn more about the Rolling Stones, please visit **abdobooklinks.com** or scan this QR code. These links are routinely monitored and updated to provide the most current information available.

More Information

For more information on this subject, contact or visit the following organizations:

Delta Blues Museum
1 Blues Alley
Clarksdale, MS 38614
662-627-6820
deltabluesmuseum.org

The Rolling Stones named themselves after a song by blues legend Muddy Waters, whose work greatly influenced their style. The Delta Blues Museum explores the history and heritage of American blues music.

Rock & Roll Hall of Fame
1100 Rock and Roll Blvd.
Cleveland, OH 44114
216-781-7625
rockhall.com

The Rock & Roll Hall of Fame features the people, events, and songs that have shaped the music world via exhibits, programs, and concerts. Its mission is to engage, teach, and inspire through the power of rock and roll.

SOURCE NOTES

CHAPTER 1. OPPORTUNITY KNOCKING

1. Richard Havers. "The Rolling Stones Play Their First Ever Gig." *uDiscoverMusic*, 12 July 2019, udiscovermusic.com. Accessed 3 Aug. 2019.

2. Christopher Sandford. "Start It Up: The 50th Anniversary of the Rolling Stones' First Gig." *Guardian*, 9 July 2012, theguardian.com. Accessed 11 Sept. 2019.

3. Sandford, "Start It Up."

4. Sandford, "Start It Up."

5. Havers, "The Rolling Stones Play Their First Ever Gig."

6. Keith Richards and James Fox. *Life*. Back Bay Books, 2011. 97.

CHAPTER 2. MUST LOVE BLUES

1. Keith Richards and James Fox. *Life*. Back Bay Books, 2011. 110.

CHAPTER 3. GETTING GIGS, COLLECTING FANS

1. Patrick Humphries. "In Search of the Rolling Stones's London Haunts." *Telegraph*, 4 Sept. 2019, telegraph.co.uk. Accessed 15 Jan. 2020.

2. Carl Arrington. "Tina Turner, the Woman Who Taught Mick Jagger to Dance, Is on the Prowl Again." *People*, 7 Dec. 1981, people.com. Accessed 28 Sept. 2019.

3. "When a Rolling Stones 1965 Dublin Concert Turned into a Riot." *IrishCentral*, 3 Sept. 2019, irishcentral.com. Accessed 15 Jan. 2020.

4. "The Beatles See the Rolling Stones Perform for the First Time." *Beatles Bible*, n.d., beatlesbible.com. Accessed 15 Jan. 2020.

5. Abe Hawken. "The Rolling Stones Go Snap, Crackle, and Pop! 1960s Commercial for Cereal Sung by the Band Is Unearthed by Incredulous Internet." *Daily Mail*, 26 July 2016, dailymail.co.uk. Accessed 15 Jan. 2020.

CHAPTER 4. ALBUMS, TOURS, AND ED SULLIVAN

1. "The Rolling Stones First Appearance on *The Ed Sullivan Show* 10/25/1964." *Ed Sullivan Show*, n.d., edsullivan.com. Accessed 15 Jan. 2020.

2. Larry Zolf. "Would You Let Your Daughter Marry a Rolling Stone?" *CBC Archives*, 14 Nov. 1965. Accessed 16 Aug. 2019.

3. Zolf, "Would You Let Your Daughter Marry a Rolling Stone?"

4. Zolf, "Would You Let Your Daughter Marry a Rolling Stone?"

5. Keith Richards and James Fox. *Life*. Back Bay Books, 2011. 263–264.

6. Steve Turner. "The Rolling Stones: A Career in Quotes." *Guardian*, 26 June 2013, theguardian.com. Accessed 15 Jan. 2020.

CHAPTER 5. BUSTED

1. "Let's Spend the Night Together." *Songfacts*, n.d., songfacts.com. Accessed 15 Jan. 2020.

2. "The Rolling Stones Chronicle 1969." *Time Is on Our Side*, n.d., timeisonourside.com. Accessed 15 Jan. 2020.

CHAPTER 6. COMMERCIAL SUCCESS

1. Robert Klara. "How Mick Jagger's Mouth Became the Rolling Stones Iconic Logo." *Adweek*, 20 July 2015, adweek.com. Accessed 24 Sept. 2019.

2. Barry Nicolson. "Rolling Stones: The Grisly Death-and-Drugs Filled Story of 'Sticky Fingers.'" *NME*, 23 Apr. 2015, nme.com. Accessed 15 Jan. 2020.

3. Michael Gallucci. "Revisiting the Rolling Stones' 70s Slide on 'Black and Blue.'" *Ultimate Classic Rock*, 22 Apr. 2016, ultimateclassicrock.com. Accessed 15 Jan. 2020.

4. Christopher R. Weingarten, David Browne, et al. "The 50 Greatest Concerts of the Last 50 Years." *Rolling Stone*, 12 June 2017, rollingstone.com. Accessed 15 Jan. 2020.

5. Weingarten, Browne, et al., "The 50 Greatest Concerts of the Last 50 Years."

6. Steve Turner. "The Rolling Stones: A Career in Quotes." *Guardian*, 26 June 2013, theguardian.com. Accessed 15 Jan. 2020.

SOURCE NOTES CONTINUED

CHAPTER 7. LIVE IN CONCERT!

1. Keith Richards and James Fox. *Life*. Back Bay Books, 2011. 415.

2. Sean O'Hagan. "The Stones and the True Story of Exile on Main Street." *Guardian*, 24 Apr. 2010, theguardian.com. Accessed 28 Aug. 2019.

3. Bryan Wawzenek. "Revisiting the Rolling Stones' Big, Bright US Tattoo You Tour." *Ultimate Classic Rock*, 25 Sept. 2016, ultimateclassicrock.com. Accessed 6 Sept. 2019.

4. Kurt Loder and Steve Pond. "Stones Tour Pays Off." *Rolling Stone*, 21 Jan. 1982, rollingstone.com. Accessed 15 Jan. 2020.

5. Michael Gallucci. "How the Rolling Stones Survived the '80s." *Ultimate Classic Rock*, 3 Nov. 2016, ultimateclassicrock.com. Accessed 15 Jan. 2020.

6. Martin Kielty. "How Keith Richards' Side Project Helped Him Appreciate Mick Jagger More." *Ultimate Classic Rock*, 14 Apr. 2019, ultimateclassicrock.com. Accessed 7 Sept. 2019.

7. Corbin Reiff. "Bill Wyman Returns Solo after 33 Years: 'I Thought, What the Hell.'" *Rolling Stone*, 22 May 2015, rollingstone.com. Accessed 7 Sept. 2019.

8. Eric Boehlert. "Rolling Stones Bring Voodoo Lounge Tour to an End." *Rolling Stone*, 22 Feb. 1996, rollingstone.com. Accessed 7 Sept. 2019.

9. Nick DeRiso. "How Rolling Stones Rediscovered Their Core with 'A Bigger Bang.'" *Ultimate Classic Rock*, 5 Sept. 2015, ultimateclassicrock.com. Accessed 7 Sept. 2019.

10. Ray Waddell. "Rolling Stones Tour Grosses More than Half a Billion." *Billboard*, 3 Oct. 2007, billboard.com. Accessed 8 Sept. 2019.

11. "Biggest Concerts of All Time." *Songkick*, 3 July 2012, blog.songkick.com. Accessed 28 Sept. 2019.

12. Larry Rohter. "The Stones Rock 1.5 Million in Rio Days before Carnival." *New York Times*, 19 Feb. 1996, nytimes.com. Accessed 28 Sept. 2019.

CHAPTER 8. THE WORLD'S GREATEST ROCK BAND

1. "The Rolling Stones Celebrate 50 Years on Stage on Anniversary of First Gig at London's Marquee Club." *New York Daily News*, 12 July 2012, nydailynews.com. Accessed 8 Aug. 2019.

2. "Pirates of the Caribbean: At World's End: Premiere Keith Richards 'Captain Teague' Interview." *YouTube*, uploaded by ScreenSlam, 16 July 2014, youtube.com. Accessed 20 Feb. 2020.

3. Patrick Oppmann. "Rolling Stones Make History with Free Concert in Cuba." *CNN*, 27 Mar. 2016, cnn.com. Accessed 29 Sept. 2019.

4. Erica Banas. "The Rolling Stones' 'No Filter' Tour Made an Obscene Amount of Money." *WMMR*, 13 Sept. 2019, wmmr.com. Accessed 29 Sept. 2019.

5. "Street Fighting Man." *Genius*, n.d., genius.com. Accessed 15 Jan. 2020.

6. James Sullivan. "Like a Rolling Stone: Bands Influenced by Mick and the Boys." *SF Gate*, 3 Nov. 2002, sfgate.com. Accessed 29 Sept. 2019.

7. Leslie Richin. "The Rolling Stones: A First-Time Listener's Guide." *Billboard*, 26 July 2017, billboard.com. Accessed 29 Sept. 2019.

8. Patrick Doyle. "50 Years Ago Today, the Rolling Stones Played Their First Gig." *Rolling Stone*, 12 July 2012, rollingstone.com. Accessed 8 Aug. 2019.

9. "Ron Wood." *IMDB*, n.d., imdb.com. Accessed 8 Sept. 2019.

INDEX

ABOUT THE AUTHOR

Jill C. Wheeler

Jill C. Wheeler is the author of more than 300 nonfiction titles for young readers. Her interests include biographies, along with the natural and behavioral sciences. She lives in Minneapolis, Minnesota, where she enjoys sailing, riding motorcycles, and reading.